What is Your Purpose?

Age like A Child

Rebbeca Grace, Evee Lea and Wendy Fischer

WestBow Press books may be ordered through booksellers or by contacting:

WestBow Press
A Division of Thomas Nelson & Zondervan
1663 Liberty Drive
Bloomington, IN 47403
www.westbowpress.com
844.714.3454

Because of the dynamic nature of the Internet, any web addresses or links contained
in this book may have changed since publication and may no longer be valid. The views
expressed in this work are solely those of the author and do not necessarily reflect the views
of the publisher, and the publisher hereby disclaims any responsibility for them.

Any people depicted in stock imagery provided by Thinkstock are models,
and such images are being used for illustrative purposes only.
Certain stock imagery © Thinkstock.

ISBN: 978-1-6642-5102-1 (sc)
ISBN: 978-1-6642-0842-1 (hc)
ISBN: 978-1-9736-1642-9 (e)

Library of Congress Control Number: 2018900289

Print information available on the last page.

WestBow Press rev. date: 11/29/2021

I'd like to dedicate this book to: Keller, Kamoni Jayce, Kallie and Kazden; each one of you are a color in my rainbow and a flower in my bouquet. My family, together with Amanda and Michelle are a ray of sunshine in every one of my days. THE LORD has so blessed me with you all. Wendy Fischer

I'd like to dedicate this book to my husband, who teaches me to be more childlike each day. Rebecca Grace

What is your

purpose?

Patience, MY dear,

you have hurdles to climb.

Aging is not an easy task.

I have greatness in store.

Wait... Seek... Find.

Opportunities galore,

choices abound.

You will see first fruits

replenish your soul.

Give ME your all,

relinquish control,

for I have all things in

the palm of MY hand.

You jump and grab,

but I AM faster

than you-am.

I think it's funny.

You do not.

This is the issue.

Wait and see what I'VE

got in store for you.

Play with ME. IAM so fun!

Come with ME,

let ME show you

how it's done!

You wear yourself ragged

doing all your deeds,

but IAM with you even

when you sneeze.

I have it all figured out here

in the palm of MY hand.

It's here for the taking

from THE GRAND IAM.

Play with ME.

See the ups and downs.

It's fun!

I have it even when

you frown.

Seek ME in all you do,

greatness will happen

in one plus a two!

Remember to

relinquish control,

for the door stays closed

to those that want more.

But to the ones that smile,

bow and give thanks,

I open it willing, and it's

there that we dance.

Sing praises to ME
you glorious child!
I await and answer to
those who will serve.

ME, high above, all

around you IAM.

Abound, come forth,
seek ME, THE
GREAT IAM.

I have you.

I have you, I do.

In the palm of MY hand

are a few things or two.

In perfect order are

things in your plan.

I'VE got this, I do.

In MY palm, it is true.

Wait and see

grandeur unfold.

Wait and see even

when you're old.

Patience, MY dear,

with your father and mum.

I guide them; they listen

to MY piper's drum.

Get on the bandwagon,

open your ear!

As things unfold, it

will be very clear.

Stay with ME.

Relinquish control.

I've got this!

I've got this!

Then merry your soul!

You Can Do Anything!

HE will take it from here.

GOD is so fun! Watch for HIM around every corner, in every crease and wrinkle in life. For all the folds straighten in due time and the journey is amazing when looking back.

Evee Lea

This is how our lives intersected with each other's throughout the culmination of this book. As we are created to worship our GREAT LORD and SAVIOR and to touch each other's lives in a way that gives HIM the glory, we do so now. This book is an example of HIS tapestry of woven threads that can only be seen when looking back. There are no coincidences.

Rebecca was 15 when we met. I could see she was different from other teenagers. That "set apart by GOD" kind of different. She was so young, beautiful, sure, solid, steadfast, confident, and unwavering in her determined spirit. As a bonus, she happens to have received a gift for editing. Who knew that her huge question and prayer about GOD's purpose for her life would unravel and pour out the words you read today?

I met a family member of Rebecca's a few times. He's the one who sent Rebecca my way. I bet he had no idea he was weaving a thread in this tapestry. No one can truly know how they are affecting the world in what seems like simple moments or chance introductions.

Then, came along delightful Kathy! She was the first to hear and the first to cheer! This gave me the courage to share these words with Laurie.

Laurie and I met 25 years ago by riding together to a museum outing: a seemingly random, chance ride. Over the years our friendship grew. I discovered her unique perspective and her heart for seeing how GOD so amazingly knits everyone together. I believe the world is a better place with her in it.

Laurie introduced me to her mother, Barbara. When I saw her smile and her heart beam, I could see how generations carry similar looks, traits, and gifts into the world. These two women made this book financially possible for you to read.

Through Laurie's husband I met John. Rebecca and I sat on this manuscript for seven years, not knowing how to get it from there to your hands. He took the time to show interest and ask questions. With gentleness and humor, he planted seeds of inspiration and motivation into this journey.

Wendy Fischer

How we unite, how THE MAKER knits our lives together, and how our actions touch others is truly amazing. In awe, Rebecca and I give thanks to you all, and to THE ALMIGHTY FATHER who weaves us all together in this moment and the moments to come.

Wendy Fischer and Rebecca Grace

REBECCA GRACE is a child of God dedicated to serving and loving His children through her dedication as a nurse, friend, wife, and dog mom.

EVEE LEA makes sure we give all the glory to The Lord, for Wendy isn't the brilliance behind the words that spilled forth.

WENDY FISCHER is from Wisconsin. She travels back and forth to Arizona writing for THE LORD, studying HIS WORD, and spending time with her daughter and grandchildren. She heads 2 Fish Worth, LLC. A Christian Ministry.

2 fish Worth

A Christian Ministry

2fishworth@gmail.com

▶ 2 Fish Worth

www.2fishworth.com

Printed in the United States
by Baker & Taylor Publisher Services